12:7
SERVE

2015-16 NMI
MISSION EDUCATION RESOURCES

❋ ❋ ❋

BOOKS

WORLD CHANGERS
MKs and Where They Are Now
By Ellen Decker

EXTREME NAZARENE
Cross-Cultural Partners in Peru
By Pat Stockett Johnston

12:7 SERVE
Global Youth Serving in Mission
By David Gonzalez and Joel Tooley, Compilers

ONCE UPON AN ISLAND
From Farming to Fiji and Papua New Guinea
By Bessie Black

REVIVAL FIRES
The Horn of Africa Story
By Howie Shute

KINGDOM ADVANCE
in South Asia and India
By Dorli Gschwandtner and Sarah Dandge

❋ ❋ ❋

NEW ADULT MISSION EDUCATION CURRICULUM
Living Mission
Where the Church Is Not Yet

12:7
SERVE
Global Youth Serving in Mission

DAVID GONZALEZ & JOEL TOOLEY
Compilers

Nazarene Publishing House
Kansas City, Missouri

Copyright © 2015 by Nazarene Publishing House
Nazarene Publishing House
PO Box 419527
Kansas City, MO 64141
www.BeaconHillBooks.com

ISBN 978-0-8341-3476-8

Printed in the
United States of America

Cover design: Jeff Gifford
Interior design: Sharon Page

The Internet addresses, email addresses, and phone numbers in
this book are accurate at the time of publication. They are provided as a resource. Nazarene Publishing House does not endorse
them or vouch for their content or permanence.

10 9 8 7 6 5 4 3 2 1

Contents

1
BICYCLES, BUSES, AND BURROS

Joel Tooley

Cars, bicycles, buses, motorcycles, burros, subways, airplanes, and a lot of walking—this is a journey of leadership and a journey of humility . . . this is a journey of urgency and a journey of patience . . . this is a journey of fame and a journey of servitude.

Sometimes, it is not fun to be in ministry.

Recently, a friend of ours who has a long history of living an intimate, worship-filled life with Christ broke the news to us that she is in a homosexual relationship with a friend of hers and is no longer serving Christ.

About the same time, a lady who is a new member of our church and was engaged in discipleship called us from the neighboring town . . . in prison. She had been arrested for trying to steal from a local store for money to support her drug relapse.

An eleven-year-old boy who indicated his desire to become a follower of Jesus during our vacation Bible school this past summer just told me he was suspended from school for physically assaulting his schoolteacher.

One step forward; two steps back. Maybe it would be better to just throw in the towel—call it quits.

But then . . .

The nine-year-old immigrant boy we met at a neighborhood apartment complex brought his non-English-speaking parents to church for the first time in his life—and in their lives, as well. The next week, he asked his Sunday school teacher, "Can you repeat what you said about needing Jesus in our lives? It sounded really important and I don't want to forget it."

Andrea, a physical trainer at the nearby gym, is living with someone in an unhealthy relationship. She heard about a Bible study my wife is leading and asked if she could join them. She came. And she returned. And returned again.

A nonbelieving businesswoman, whose path intersects with mine each month at the local chamber of commerce meeting, asked if I would pray for an important issue in her life.

"Paaassttoooor!" I barely heard the excited scream before nearly being tackled by the hugging kindergartner when she saw me on her school campus. Brittany, who recently reunited with her mom after spending three years in foster care, became a follower of Jesus when she gave her heart to God during our vacation Bible school.

The journey of ministry is like any other aspect of life—it's filled with highs and lows, ups and downs, ebbs and flows. However, it's important to note that ministry to others, in its richest form, is when we take the form of a servant as Scripture guides us in Philippians 2:5-7:

In your relationships with one another, have the same mindset as Christ Jesus: Who, being in very nature God, did not consider equality with God something to be used to his own advantage; rather, he made himself nothing by taking the very nature of a servant, being made in human likeness. And being found in appearance as a man, he humbled himself by becoming obedient to death—even death on a cross! Therefore God exalted him to the highest place and gave him the name that is above every name, that at the name of Jesus every knee should bow, in heaven and on earth and under the earth, and every tongue acknowledge that Jesus Christ is Lord, to the glory of God the Father.

After a small group of junior-high-aged teenagers and I had a time of discipleship, we headed over to a local restaurant to indulge in "bottomless" chips and salsa. The server's face expressed her obvious lack of joy in being assigned to our table—especially when these frugal teens all ordered ice water (with lemon, of course). Apparently, this particular group silently screamed to her, "You won't earn a huge tip from us!"

She served us accordingly.

It has happened before—young punk kids noisily enter a restaurant; they order the cheapest food possible and make a huge mess. Then, they walk out without leaving much—if any—of a tip for the server. A lot of work with little return.

I confess: Sometimes I feel like that waitress. I just "know" the people I'm about to serve will not show any appreciation for my hard work. Even worse, sometimes I imagine that they'll actually disapprove of my work.

I wonder what would happen if every missionary, every pastor, every youth leader, every [fill-in-the-blank] would take on the experience of working as a server in a restaurant. Since it seems like restaurant servers are working for the big tip, maybe that experience could also be helpful for people going into ministry.

You see—typically, the tip is based on the amount of money the customer spends on food and beverages. If a customer orders expensive food and expensive beverages, some servers tend to give a little more personalized attention. The opposite tends to be true too. In this scenario, the generalization would mean that perhaps less attention is given to those who will presumably offer little in return.

That's simply not at the heart of what it means to take on the form of a servant.

So, the idea of creating an internationally cross-cultural team of twelve young adults from seven areas of the world came with the notion that this particular group of missionaries should stand out in a markedly different style. This team—the 12:7 Serve team—should bear an indelible mark that would be lived out as a distinct model and a reminder to those who have gone before them and for those who would follow . . . this notion of ministering as a servant.

What you will read in the following pages are accounts of how God—our serving God—

shaped, equipped, and empowered twelve unique missionaries to develop and use their gift of serving—and ultimately used those acts of service to make Christlike disciples in the nations.

- Kesner Absolu—Port au Prince, Haiti (Mesoamerica Region)
- Danielle (Dani) Castlehow—Perth, Australia (Asia-Pacific Region)
- Erika Chaves—San Pedro de Poás, Costa Rica (Mesoamerica Region)
- AJ Fry—Olathe, Kansas (USA/Canada Region)
- Helen Herrera—San José, Costa Rica (Mesoamerica Region)
- Alan Hernandez—Chihuahua, Mexico (Mesoamerica Region)
- Carlos Jimenez—Puebla, Mexico (Mesoamerica Region)
- Chennice McClean—Perth, Scotland (Eurasia Region)
- Maura Narvaez—León, Nicaragua (Mesoamerica Region)

- Estela Reza—Shawnee, Kansas (USA/Canada Region)
- Janary (Jana) Suyat de Godoy—Manila, Philippines (Asia-Pacific Region)
- Lynda Woolford—Georgetown, Guyana (Mesoamerica Region)

These twelve servants completed a rigorous application process and were selected to participate in this ministry, sponsored by Nazarene Youth International and the Youth Mobilization ministry of the Mesoamerica Region. They served throughout the Mesoamerica Region in the countries of:

- St. Kitts and Nevis (English/Dutch Field)
- Haiti (French Field)
- Dominican Republic (Mesoamerica Central Field)
- Guadalajara, Mexico (Mexico North Field)
- Chiapas, Mexico (Mexico South Field)
- Guatemala/El Salvador (CA-4 Field)

- Panama City, Panama (Mesoamerica Central Field)

Cars, bicycles, buses, motorcycles, burros, subways, airplanes, and a lot of walking—this was a journey of leadership and a journey of humility. Beaches, churches, hospitals, orphanages, schools, child development centers, and slums—this was a journey of urgency and a journey of patience. Sunday school classrooms, city parks, JESUS Film showings, nursing homes, and national auditoriums—this was a journey of fame and a journey of servitude.

"If your gift is serving others, serve them well" (Rom. 12:7, NLT).

Joel Tooley
12:7 Serve Project Onsite Coordinator

2

AN ENORMOUS CLOCK
God Uses Everyone
Carlos Jimenez, Mexico

One of my all-time favorite movies is Disney's *The Incredibles*. My favorite character is Edna Mode because, although she is small in size, she is a great woman—and she is very funny.

Edna Mode pulls Elastigirl together and encourages her to confront the problem; to fight and win!

Seriously, if you haven't seen that movie, put this book down and don't come back until you have watched it. Well, maybe we should keep reading instead. I don't want to get us distracted.

I was thinking of that movie because besides the fact that I love it, one other scene can help us understand the idea of this chapter a little better. Mr. Huph and Bob Parr are talking and Mr. Huph explains that their company is like an enormous clock; that it only works if all the little clogs mesh together. He points out that a clock needs to be cleaned, well lubricated, and wound tight. It needs to have intricate parts that fit and cooperate together as they're supposed to.

When we talk about the church, we can think in this same way. Just like with Mr. Huph's company, each of us has a specific task to do in order to complete our mission.

Our mission: To make Christlike disciples in the nations. However, we often don't know what our job is. Am I a cog or a spring? Should I teach the children or clean the benches? Is God calling me to preach or play the guitar?

Sometimes we see so many possibilities that we don't know where to start; yet at other times we don't see any possibilities of what we can do and end up doing nothing but being frustrated and asking, "God, why did You call me?"

If you've been in this situation, please raise your hand.

Thanks. Now I know I'm not the only one.

When the 12:7 Serve project started in October 2011, the team members were introduced to each other virtually. We were asked to write a brief biography so we could start to have an idea of who we would live with for the next six months.

Little by little, the documents started to appear on our private Facebook group page. As I read my teammates' biographies, and especially when I read about their current ministries, I started to think, *Oh man! These people are amazing! They have all this experience and preparation and they've gone through amazing moments with the Lord and I've got nothing! They don't seem to need me at all!*

Months passed quickly as we prepared and February 2012 came—the day when we finally met in person. During all of this time, the idea of "I'm the weak one in the group" kept growing in my mind. To my surprise, when we were talking and sweating in the delightful Panama heat during that first day, we all confessed to feeling the same way!

We humans usually focus on what we see others do and it's probably because we're having the same problem Samuel the prophet had when he was looking for a king to replace Saul: "But GOD told Samuel, 'Looks aren't everything. Don't be impressed with his looks and stature. . . . GOD judges persons differently than humans do. Men and women look at the face; GOD looks into the heart'" (1 Sam. 16:7, TM).

We are so used to judging things through our human perspective that it is easy to forget that when we come before God, nothing is about what we can do, but about what He can do through us. He wants to take the gifts and talents He has given us and do incredible things. And the only thing He is looking for is a willing heart.

It might be difficult, but we need to stop thinking we have nothing to offer, stop looking "at the face," and let God work.

Beginning with our first day in Panama, and lasting throughout the following months of our journey, God worked with all of us, demonstrating what He is capable of doing. Every day, He was teaching us that He has a job for everyone who's willing to follow Him. *Everyone*. Even in a team of twelve.

Remember that phrase, "Two heads are better than one"?

We learned that phrase is not valid anymore, when you have twelve heads! It is not easy to organize twelve people to do something, even when they are from the same country and culture. Now imagine what it's like with nine nationalities and twelve different cultures involved!

But again, God had a place for each of us. He wasn't paying attention to our knowledge or to what our appearances were like. He didn't even care about the country we came from. He was looking at our hearts.

Because of the nature of the team—twelve leaders—many of us were familiar with and comfortable engaging in the assignments we were asked to do during the trip: evangelism, children's ministry, preaching, and leading worship.

However, not everyone was comfortable with everything. I tried to avoid preaching a couple of times. And every time we were asked to lead in worship, no one wanted to be the leading voice.

Nevertheless, we did the uncomfortable jobs anyway and when we did, we discovered that even though most of those things still weren't our preferences, a couple of them did become our new favorites. I'm still not very comfortable preaching, but I know I can do it. At the same time, I've noticed I love to translate in workshops or for somebody who is preaching. I never would have discovered that without trying new things, even when I was afraid to do it.

I cannot imagine a different 12:7 Serve team. Each member brought something special to our family, making our ministry varied and more effective. Allow me to remind you once more: This did not happen because of us! It was all because God taught us to not look at ourselves and what others around us are doing, but to see what He could do with a willing heart.

You might be thinking, "Great, He's looking at my heart. I still don't know what my call is!"

As I told you, I was once lost . . . but now I'm found. I mean I was once lost on what my role was in church. Being a pastor's kid gave me the opportunity to see a lot of ministries and to have a good idea of how a church works, in the administrative area at least.

Seeing and watching are not the same thing as experiencing. I could spend my life watching others evangelize, teach the kids, work with teenagers, or do any other "church stuff," but I can never know what my calling is until I go and actually do something.

My recommendation? I have two. Ask your pastor what you can do in your church to help serve—he or she will be happy to know you want to help—and get involved in missions.

"Missions? Why missions?"

If this is what you are asking, I want to ask you, "Why not?"

A lifestyle of missions holds a huge opportunity to develop or even discover your gifts and talents. That doesn't necessarily mean that you will become a career missionary. But since missions opportunities are as diverse as the people we minister to, you'll find that you can try many different ministries and experience many things that God can use to let you know where you can serve in His church.

A good example of how God uses you even though you are not sure about your gifts is the story of Lolita, a shy young girl from Mexico.

When our 12:7 Serve team was in Ichan (a small town), we divided into smaller groups. My group included this young girl Lolita, Danielle (from Australia), and me. We planned a puppet show for the children, and Lolita was terrified of being a part of it. But she did it and afterward, she also prayed for the very first time with a person who decided to follow Jesus. She was very excited and now she is leading Sunday school every week with the children in Ichan.

Whether you are a leader with a lot of experience or you're just beginning to walk in this area, keep one thing in mind: No matter what the task is, if God is calling you to do it, He will guide you and empower you.

Just keep a willing heart and open ears to His voice and He will show you the way. It might be terrifying to think about what you need to do. Perhaps it's your first time, you might not want to do it, or you don't even know what to do. But whatever the case, be courageous, try new things, dare yourself to go beyond your comfort zone, and leave your worries in the Lord's hands.

Here are some questions for us to consider:

- Who can help me discover and use my spiritual gifts and God-given talents?
- How do I view myself? What does God's Word teach me about His view of who He created me to be?
- Am I avoiding something God has asked me to do? Why?

- Is there any ministry opportunity that I've never been involved in and could try?

Remember, He has some incredible places for you to serve!

3
UNITY VS. UNIFORMITY
Teamwork
Janary Suyat de Godoy, Philippines

Every time I pass the music conservatory of one university in Manila, I hear the beautiful sounds of different instruments being played. When I first learned about the place, I intentionally walked near it hoping I would hear a violin, flute, or other instrument playing a nice solo piece. Instead, I heard different instruments playing at the same time, coming from different rooms, playing different music scores.

This actually made me want to walk faster and get away, since it sounded like chaos to me. However, we are all aware that when these instruments come together to form an orchestra and all play their parts in one beautifully arranged musical score, they create a great harmony that lures us in and stirs our emotions.

A beautiful harmony moves us.

This image filled my mind when our 12:7 Serve team was at our third site, the Dominican Republic. I was sitting with the team during a meeting inside the work and witness house in Santo Domingo, wondering how someone came up with an idea to bring together twelve youth from different countries: two were from the United States; two from Costa Rica; two from Mexico; and one each from Guyana, Haiti, Australia, Scotland, Nicaragua, and the Philippines.

The twelve youth from different regions with different cultures and personalities were sitting in that meeting trying to work things out because we had noticed that we were different from each other and had been trying to make our "own different sounds."

We came to a point when we were trying to figure out the word "harmony." I told myself, "We are an explosion of differences with tendencies to do our own things, in our own different ways."

A Swahili proverb says: "A boat doesn't go forward if each one is rowing their own way." I thought maybe the team needed to discuss how to be "one."

My time with 12:7 Serve taught me a lot about *teamwork*. This is a common concept that's definitely hard to practice. We all know how difficult it is to not do things our own way; it is interesting that our team worked, for that is a wonderful example of the body of Christ.

The team had meetings every once in a while to review the service we were doing and in one of those meetings, a team member said: "If we do not work as a team, the people we are serving can sense it; they can notice that something is not right."

That statement made sense to me. It is possible for us to serve the people and the community around us individually, but what testimony do we have when we are not serving as one body and each person wants to have his or her own

28

way? Surely it will be chaotic and will affect the team members' relationships with each other.

This reminds me of the song, "They will know we are Christians by our love." This refers to our love for one another; being united just as Jesus told His disciples that they should love one another.

At this essential point at our third site, when all hearts were vulnerable and open, we started to talk about things we did not like, or behaviors that irritated us. We reflected that before we could serve others, we needed to be able to serve each other well. We had to be there for each other. We realized that the people we minister to noticed whether or not we served as one body or were divided.

The team came up with goals and talked about what we could do to build our relationships with each other. We talked about intentionally encouraging each other.

We did not even notice time pass as we spent three hours of what became a very important talk for our team.

We all prayed for each other and asked the Holy Spirit to fill us and make us one. We are all a part of the family of God; we are His children and we all have the same Father! In Ephesians 4:1-6, the apostle Paul wrote to the Ephesian church:

> As a prisoner for the Lord, then, I urge you to live a life worthy of the calling you have received. Be completely humble and gentle; be patient, bearing with one another in love. Make every effort to keep the unity of the Spirit through the bond of peace. There is one body and one Spirit, just as you were called to one hope when you were called; one Lord, one faith, one baptism; one God and Father of all, who is over all and through all and in all.

Nurturing relationships is the key to teamwork. It is interesting how Paul instructs the Ephesians, and even us today, to "make every effort to keep the unity of the Spirit through the bond of peace."

How can we achieve such unity? The previous verses tell us the ingredients to unity: being completely humble and gentle, patient, and bearing with one another in love.

All these words remind me of Jesus. The Bible tells us that Jesus was full of the Spirit, and this is the Spirit that I have received—the same Spirit that my teammates and all the believers have received. No matter what skin color, race, personality, or culture each person has, we are each recipients of God's grace and the gift of the Holy Spirit, who makes us one.

Just as Christ, who was filled with the Spirit, humbled himself and came to serve and love even to the point of death, we should also put our brothers and sisters in front of our own desires and comforts.

This is so hard and painful to do, but through the Holy Spirit, we can! Not only do we come together to work, but our main goal is to love each other while we make our relationships to each other our priority.

It was interesting for me to see how the 12:7 Serve team grew from "this is me, this is what I like," to "I want to serve you."

While I would not say that we ever arrived at perfection, we moved forward. We needed many reminders to be able to do it. We were thankful for our devotions that kept bringing the team back to the example of the Living Word!

This relationship leads us into the bigger family we have outside of our team; the global church we are all part of. We may all be different, but we all belong to one family with God as our Father. We do not necessarily have to look alike or act the same way. We celebrate our differences as God's creativity in giving us different personalities, different strengths, and different gifts.

Teamwork does not mean uniformity but knowing that in our differences we all have a common purpose. We should focus on what our individual strengths can do as we follow Jesus' commission to "go and make disciples of all nations," and experience His promise with it: "and surely I am with you always, to the very end of the age" (Matt. 28:19, 20).

I believe this is not just for some, but He is with all of us. In order for us to be able to take part in our Lord's mission, His Spirit works in us, guiding us to be likeminded.

Many times, while the team was traveling, I used that time to thank God for the people who supported me so I could follow God's call for my life. I reflected how many people all over the world were praying for our team and me.

I realized that we twelve youth were not the only ones taking part in this mission trip to seven sites throughout the Mesoamerica Region. People all over the world had participated by praying, giving, and supporting us, so in a sense, they went too. With this in mind, I realized we are a few of the many pieces that make the whole, and each part is as great as the other part. We are all important in the body of Christ.

I reminded myself that God touched His children's hearts to give so the 12:7 Serve team could raise the funds for this mission. It is important to remember that the team could eat and had places to rest because God's children were gifted with hospitality and accommodated us. It is important to remember that when some of the team were waiting for visas, God's children prayed for us and sought God's will. These things are not yet the whole picture, but I believe God's children from different regions and countries could use their gifts to build the body of Christ in this mission.

I felt privileged to see the 12:7 Serve team at work making disciples in the different Mesoamerica sites where we served. At first I observed how each member was trying to figure out what to do, but as time went by, the members' gifts became evident—some were passionate in talking to people in the streets, some taught the children, some were gifted in leading worship and sharing music, some showed gifts in languages and interpretation, some showed gifts in discipleship, and some showed gifts in preaching and exhorting.

Some of the members did not even notice they could do these things. As time passed, the team members knew the parts they did best and naturally played those parts—as a single instrument in a beautiful ensemble.

As the team was sensitive to the Spirit's leading and was available, we saw the work the Holy Spirit accomplished. And it was a marvel to see how some of our team members have a blessed gift of encouragement that blessed us all during hardships, troubles, and moments when we were all tired and discouraged.

I recently read how the V-formation of geese flying south actually helps their group move faster. When one of them falls out of place, it becomes difficult for that goose to fly alone. Not only that, but geese at the back also honk to those in front as encouragement to the geese to keep flying fast.

May the geese remind us that as we all have different parts in the body of Christ and work according to our varying gifts, each one is an important part of the whole! May we learn how to encourage each other because when we are building each other, we can work as one and accomplish our mission better.

I believe that the experiences we had with our 12:7 Serve team are the same that are happening to every youth group in every church and group around the world. Even to those who speak the same language or come from the same country, differences will always be evident. It is such a good thought that God is so creative that in our different personalities and different cultures, we are able to bring something new to our team. Just as the body is made up of different parts, our differences help us complement each other. As a community of believers, we need each other and we are not meant to do the mission alone.

Take time to thank the Lord for the unique way He created you. When you notice the differences in others, don't let it be a source of criticism, but let it be an opportunity to learn something new. Let their different abilities be maximized to fulfill the mission. Thank God that you are not alone in this journey.

Do you feel you are not an important part of your group? May you be encouraged that the group can do more with you in it. You are valuable! The team is not complete without you! Are you willing for the Lord to use you in ways you have not imagined? The Holy Spirit will be with you!

Ask the Holy Spirit to fill you and help you love your brothers and sisters in the Lord so your harmony will be sweet music in the places you are called to serve.

4

WHAT WOULD YOUR REPORT CARD SAY?
Faithfulness
Lynda Woolford, Guyana

I sat dazed. My mind was blank, and I had forgotten everything I'd ever known about every nerve and organ of the body. I was in the middle of my anatomy examination and couldn't recall the slightest thing the lecturer was hinting. She kept gently prodding her lower back, while staring at me as if to suggest, "You know this!"

However, I did not know it. In fact, I was hoping she would just give up and let me leave the room. This was another year and another exam I had promised myself to study for—but I'd only picked up my book two days before my examination.

She finally let me go, and I will never forget that pain. But in that moment my perspective on preparation and work changed.

I am sure you have had those report card moments: The moment when you were either elated because you had almost perfect scores, or the moment when you felt apprehension because you knew your mother or father would give you a lecture on improving your grades and paying more attention in school.

I have had those excruciating moments, and my resolve has always been the same.

"Next term, I will work harder and begin studying as soon as I get my notes," I have promised myself. But my resolutions seldom lasted long. I rushed at the end, had sleepless nights, and made the same resolutions again.

Whether we make plans or resolutions to serve God, or only spend a few minutes doing something for Him, God still expects us to serve Him. But what if God is examining our service? What if He prepared a report card and measured your faithfulness, hard work, and stewardship? What grade would you get? Would you pass or fail?

Let's look at what it means to faithfully serve God and consider three main areas that determine whether we are being faithful servants.

Stewardship

A steward is someone who takes good care of what he or she is entrusted with—someone who manages time, resources, gifts, and abilities well.

The Bible gives us an idea of what it means to be a good steward. It means to be faithful in the job you are given (1 Cor. 4:2) and doing the job well (Col. 3:23).

Stewardship also means working well when your leaders or superiors are not around (Luke 12:41-42). So stewardship means faithfully getting the task done for the honor and glory of God at all times, even when no one is around.

Faith

Some of us on the team needed visas to travel to different countries. We felt the anxiety of waiting for the visas. But one person who stood out to me the most during that process was Absolu.

His jubilant outlook permeated his faith in God. Even when he needed to wait on a lengthy visa process, he wore a cheerful smile. The assurance of God's call upon his life and his willingness to follow God caused him—regardless of the wait, the challenges, the bus rides, and the times alone—to smile and believe that since God had called him to serve for six months in seven countries with 12:7 Serve, then God would make that possible.

I particularly remember leaving him in Mexico while he waited on his visa for El Salvador. I was saddened that he would not be on the bus rides with us. As I hugged him good-bye and boarded the bus, he said, "Are you sad, my friend . . . don't be sad. I will see you soon."

He smiled, hugged me again, and in his bubbly fashion, energetically waved good-bye to us. Sure enough, we were reunited with Absolu in El Salvador.

His approach to work and ministry was always, "I may not have this now, but because God has called me I know He will provide it."

His attitude allowed him to press on and plan and prepare for the next step because he knew that God would provide all the visas for him. Absolu's faith in God makes him stand out as a faithful servant.

God wants us to have this same faith as we approach ministry. We're not only to be faithful servants when we serve in capacities we are comfortable with or when we have all the resources we need. And He doesn't want us to have faith only when we can see the outcomes.

Our being faithful servants is most evident when we can't see where God is leading us and we don't have everything we need to get the task done. Then we can only serve because God empowers us and we know God has our back. So even when we don't have the answers to the hows, whys, and whens, just because we know that God told us to follow, we are willing to go. That is faith!

The writer of Hebrews points us to great examples of faith, reminding us that we are in excellent company. He then says to keep our eyes fixed on Jesus so we will not get tired and discouraged (Heb. 12:2-3).

This is why faith is so important in a faithful servant's life. It keeps us going when we get tired; it keeps us focused when we don't have everything; and it keeps our eyes on the ministry instead of what we don't have and we cannot do.

So do not stop or become discouraged because you do not see all the resources, but continue to express joy and the belief that God will bring the resources at the right time. Don't let the feelings of insecurity keep you from stepping out on a limb for God; but walk in the assurance that God's strength is perfect.

With our eyes on Jesus, let us reflect the obedience of Abraham, the confidence of Joshua, and the intimacy of Moses, because we know God is with us. And, let us personalize the Apostle Paul's words and jubilantly proclaim, "[I am] confident of this, that he who began a good work in [me] will carry it on to completion until the day of Christ Jesus" (Phil. 1:6).

Hard Work

When I think about hard work, I remember arduous days in the sun lifting stones with Chennice, Helen, AJ, Danielle, and Absolu in Haiti to build gardens. We experienced physical exhaustion, thirst, and fatigue.

Then there was the time in the Central District of Panama, when we were scraping paint off the walls at the manse. My hands were tender and blistered, but I felt a sense of satisfaction and accomplishment.

While these are clear examples of hard work, hard work can also mean having the determination and diligence to pursue ministry and our tasks so that God can get the glory.

With diligence and determination Maura, Kesner, and Luz responded to their task of discipleship in Chahuites, Mexico. They set out each morning to disciple new converts who had given their lives to Christ after the evangelistic thrust of the Maximum Mission the previous weekend. Maximum Mission is what we called our projects when we went out to a community to serve and do evangelism through VBS and the JESUS Film.

With their Bibles, discipleship material, and expectant hearts, these three walked about one km. every day. When they approached the first home, the door was closed and so they went to the second house. At this home, they were delighted to be greeted by the children but were disappointed to learn the mother was not at home for them to start the classes. As they continued from house to house, they were continually disappointed by the trend of closed doors. In one instance, they were excited to see one of the people arrive home but were further discouraged when the person wouldn't answer the door.

Instead of giving up, Maura, Kesner, and Luz continued those daily treks to the homes, knocking at doors and rearranging schedules but never giving up on their commitment to disciple. The mantra "Don't give up on others because Jesus never gave up on you" prodded them on until they were able to begin discipleship classes with some of the people.

Sometimes we think hard work is only evident when we have blistered hands or a tired body. But hard work is also evident in our commitment to finish a task. The experiences of Maura, Kesner, and Luz remind us that God calls us to work hard to complete the task before us. So in the words of the Apostle Paul in Philippians 3:14, let our mantra be to "press on."

Suppose you were to receive a grade for your faithfulness to God based on your stewardship, hard work, and diligence, what grade would you get?

Would God say, "Well done, my good and faithful servant" (Matt. 25:21, NLT), or would He say, "Depart from me; I do not know you" (see 7:23)?

And if you did pass, would it be a pass of distinction?

If we all commit to ministering as if we are standing before God at the end of the day waiting for our grade, how would that encourage us to minister differently?

So, what will your report card say?

5
BLESSINGS IN DISGUISE
Serving in Hardship and Victory
Erika Chaves, Costa Rica

Generally, society equates blessings with the bank statement, how good our retirement and health insurance is, or the place where we live. It is easy to forget that God blesses us with many other things—sometimes things we don't even think are there, such as fresh air every day, the sun that warms us, the waves of the sea, and other things.

While we served in the Mesoamerica Region, we could not always see the blessings or identify the precise moment they occurred. But without a doubt, the same day that the twelve members of the team knew each other personally, February 23, 2012, in the city of Panama, blessings were present behind every greeting and smile.

This journey was more than a confirmation of a missionary calling. It was an encounter with God, in which we lived out our faith and lived by faith, and our lives were transformed. We believe it ignited many children, youth, and adults around us.

The first blessing in disguise that comes to my mind is when we were living in St. Kitts, a beautiful Caribbean island filled with kind and friendly people who needed God. On this island we faced many challenges: getting to know each other as a team, figuring out how to organize ourselves and use our gifts and talents, and determining how to administer our financial resources. That is where we saw the astounding hand of God at work.

St. Kitts has very expensive food because most food products are imported. When we arrived on the island, we went to the supermarket and, based on our budget, wrote the menu and bought the items. One morning for breakfast, we had only nine eggs for thirteen people—yes, less than one egg per person! Even though it was not easy, each of us enjoyed breakfast and the grace of God showed as our hunger disappeared. God is faithful!

Another story occurred while we were serving in Haiti. This challenge was different and intense. The language (French Creole) was a major barrier, the food was also very different, and we had little access to technology.

Nevertheless, the blessing to serve in this place marked each of our lives. Our blessing began with the welcome we received at our first home and our outstanding driver, Colson, who served with us as our father, doctor, protector, guide, interpreter, and evangelist.

In the second Haitian district we visited, we slept in the church classrooms. We were always exhausted at night after a long day of work in the warm climate. But there we experienced God's presence through the words of a wonderful woman, the pastor's wife.

The night we left she explained the joy of having us and, while the tears ran down her cheeks, she told us about difficulties they'd been going through. In that moment we saw the love of Christ for her children and the fulfillment of the promise, "And everyone who has left houses or brothers or sisters or father or mother or wife or children or fields for my sake will receive a hundred times as much and will inherit eternal life" (Matt. 19:29). Without a doubt we experienced God's blessing in every smile and prayer from that amazing woman.

As the weeks passed and we worked in various places, we began to miss our families and homes. And we were physically exhausted.

My birthday was approaching and I was not expecting a big celebration since that week the team would separate to serve in several places at once.

I arrived to the house that was assigned to us, the home of Pastor Jose and Martita, in Mezcala, Jalisco, north of Mexico. Their house was beautiful, but best of all was that I had a huge, comfortable bed to myself. On the day of my birthday! The best gift I could receive was to sleep so well in the home of this generous family, waking up the next morning being thankful to God for the thoughtful gift of sleep. It was a simple but loving blessing in disguise.

A blessing we enjoyed when we least expected it happened in the Southern District of El Salvador. After the long hour drive in the back of a pickup truck, under the hot sun, some of us wanted to say, "No more."

Yet, the strength and extra motivation came after prayer and before the evangelistic activity of that day. My group that morning included AJ and Chennice. We went to knock on the doors of the neighborhood homes, but it seemed that no one wanted to hear about Jesus.

On our way back, the church leader asked that we visit a woman with various problems—her husband and one son were alcoholics, and her other son was imprisoned. We walked to her house and the woman offered us a seat on her patio; a humble home, made of clay. After we talked with her for some time, she expressed her need of Christ, but told us she was afraid to attend church because her husband would not like that.

While she told us about her husband's impulsive temperament, we heard the front gate open. It was her husband! A little frightened, we greeted him and tried to carry on the conversation, waiting for this man to insult us. But after a few minutes, the man became part of the conversation, seeking to be helped. When we asked if they wanted to receive Jesus in their hearts both replied, "Yes."

What a special moment—seeing lives transformed, even if our bodies and the scorching sun had been telling us it was time to rest. That night this couple attended the church service. With a smile, they said, "Thank you for visiting us today; we needed it."

Definitely a blessing we didn't expect.

We saw more examples of God's faithfulness with every detail—how we always had enough toothpaste, the insurmountable ounces of insect repellent that never ran out, the meals we always had, the "adoptive" parents that God provided in every place. In the end, countless blessings, whether in times of comfort and laughter or scarcity and sorrow. God's blessings were always present; disguised sometimes, but always there in the appropriate time and place.

In retrospect, I am convinced that God created every person in order to include him or her in His perfect and redemptive work in the world. And when He brought us to the Mesoamerica Region, twelve young people from different places and cultures, to serve with that mission in mind, He also promised to be with us. What greater blessing could we ask for? Not only did we have many blessings, but we also experienced the biggest blessing of all: the Giver of blessings.

Without a doubt, during the time we ministered in the project 12:7 Serve, we learned that blessings are intimately related to our obedience and commitment to serve.

Christianity is reflected in the practical meaning of that word: "serve." We read about that practical service in James 1:27, "Religion that God our Father accepts as pure and faultless is this: to look after orphans and widows in their distress and to keep oneself from being polluted by the world."

When we are ready to serve—either in comfort or in moments of difficulty—God's goodness will be present in each moment. He will guide us toward His blessings. And in a similar way to His care for us during the six months of the project, He has also promised that He will guide us and bless us wherever we are a part of His mission. Yes, because our "field missionary" also can be our family, our neighborhood, our school, our workplace, our town, and so forth. But the most important thing is that we trust Him, responding to His call with obedience and faithfulness.

The life of holiness and service does not mean doing the most remarkable, noteworthy things, but loving God with all that we are and fully trusting Him.

So keep moving forward! We will not give up, knowing that the greatest blessings appear in unexpected ways—and perhaps even "disguised."

6

FLEXIBILITY IS THE KEY

Janary Suyat de Godoy, Philippines

I had just finished my class when I opened an email from our regional NYI coordinator. He told me about a mission opportunity for the newly combined Mexico/Central America Region, which was called the Mesoamerica Region.

I was taking a class on history of missions at the seminary during that time and had been asking the Lord how He would unfold His missionary call for my life. I had read a lot of stories about how God sent different people to the mission field and how He had stretched their faith.

I was filled with excitement as I read the email. I visited the website that showed the information for the 12:7 Serve missions opportunity. Then the excitement turned into worries, and my head filled with questions:

- I read that the team would go to seven different sites, and I suddenly thought of the seven visa applications I would need to fill out.

- I would need to raise about USD2,000 for the project, not including round-trip airfare to the other side of the world.

- I would have less than six months to complete all of these requirements before the project started.

- I would have to make many changes to my personal plans in order to join the project.

Everything inside me was convinced that this was "mission impossible." However, nothing is impossible with God! This was just the beginning of God stretching me in the many areas of my life.

It is actually funny to recall my teammates' versions of "how it all started" for them. Some of them had to quit jobs, give up many things, and go through many changes. I guess it is funny looking back now at the tough situations that have passed, but many tears were shed during the trying times. Some of us did not even think we would finish the project—but God is faithful and saw us through.

We have always heard the cliché, "The only thing constant is change."

I have learned that not all people can easily cope with change, but as we have seen in history, changes happen, and people need to adapt to their new situations to survive. I think we can say that being flexible is essential and a quality that we should all desire. Gailey and Culbertson, in the book *Discovering Missions*, noted that being flexible is "a good characteristic to have in cross-cultural mission."

The other thing I have learned is how some people like to make plans and how some people just go with the flow. Our team usually met daily to write an agenda of the things we needed to do. Imagine the surprise many of us felt when we could not control what was happening in the program! I am not sure if most of us felt this way but some of us (especially me) get really frustrated when we can't control situations. Maybe some of you would faint at the thought of seeing things not happening as planned.

When we were in St. Kitts, we planned the Maximum Mission project in one site, only to find out the next day that a race was happening in the town—only two kids showed up to our children's program.

While it is important to plan the day and lay out our goals, I have learned after many frustrating days, to include these words in my to-do list for the day: "be flexible, not everything will turn out the way you planned it," along with a smiley face.

I was not like this before many of our experiences. It was interesting to see the mix of frustration, encouragement, and laughter that my teammates have shown through changes. After we'd been together for several months, we could joke about how things don't always go as planned, and we have become great at going impromptu!

Maura and I were in the Dominican Republic when we went several times to the Mexican embassy to process our visas to Mexico. The approval process was taking a long time. The team had to leave the Dominican Republic, and we still had no news of the visas. We were told that there was a Plan B for us if our Mexican visas were denied.

The day came when they flew to Mexico and we were left behind. We were crying, like a family being separated, and we were feeling sorry because we wouldn't be with them for a month and a half in Mexico.

We moved to Plan B a few days before the team left for Mexico, and that was: Maura and I would go to Guatemala. Our leaders said if Plan B would not work out, it was nice to know we could still have Plan C, D, E, and so on until we finish all the letters of the alphabet!

Guatemala was not really part of the 12:7 Serve sites, but this Plan B turned out to be a blessing in disguise. Maura and I only waited for thirty minutes to get our visas at the Guatemalan embassy! I still did not have my visa to El Salvador, but when we got to the El Salvador embassy and we showed them my passport, they saw the Guatemalan visa and said that was enough for me to enter the CA-4 (Central America-4) countries: Guatemala, Honduras, El Salvador, and Nicaragua.

God was full of surprises concerning all the visa issues for me. I left the Philippines with just an approved visa to Haiti and the Dominican Republic—but God was working on the situation even though I couldn't see it! Maura and I were granted the visas to Mexico and were able to join the team already there.

The great encouragement to learn was that even though things go out of control for us, God is still in control. That is such a comfort when we feel like falling apart and losing our hope. When we dwell on our new, scary, and challenging situations more than the promises of God, who is able to give us all we can ask or imagine, we give the enemy a space to fill our heads with doubts until we can't carry on.

We stayed in a city called Santiago while we were in the Dominican Republic waiting for our visas. The churches prayed with us, and what joy for the whole church to hear that our prayers were answered! God used our stories to encourage the churches that through their prayers "in all things God works for the good of those who love him, who have been called according to his purpose" (Rom. 8:28).

When the changing situations, hardships, difficulties, and storms of life come, we always have to remember that with Jesus in our boats of life, we can smile at the storm. This is one of my favorite songs and lessons we taught the children. We also made paper boats for the kids to take home so they could remember God was with them.

Well, except for one time in Haiti it didn't work out as well. While we were eager to teach this lesson to kids in one district, in the middle of the Bible story, Colson, our friend, driver, and interpreter, told us the kids said they didn't know what a storm was or what a boat was because they had never seen the sea or experienced storms!

Helen, one of our team members assigned to help me teach, felt ill at this time and had to go rest. I felt like all the kids were staring at me thinking I was some crazy person talking about storms and boats.

A moment like this can teach us how sometimes in ministry, we can get into the danger of staying in our comfort zones. We can say, "We have done this before and it works" or "This is how we do it" or "We have done it always like this." As a result, we stop growing and trying new things.

Situations like this teach us that when we become flexible, we also grow. And we learn challenges can show us new and exciting things. When we get stuck in our comfort zones, we may get so that we can't communicate effectively anymore and even miss the point of why we are doing things.

I saw God stretch our faith and teach us to be flexible with our plans and our methods. But I also saw that our patience needed to be stretched.

Don't you just thank God for rest days? Our team got our assigned days of rest every week, but I remember one time when we traveled to different districts every three days. So much happened with so many exciting things and wonderful people for us to see and minister to. While people tend to complain, I admired the team's patience as we went to five districts. My team members adjusted their schedules and moved their Skype dates with families and friends to the last day of our stay on the site. When the last day arrived, you could see the eagerness to sleep in and to do laundry, as we always did this during our rest days. People were also excited to talk to their families.

Then the announcement came. Someone had made a mistake about the time our bus was leaving. We would have to leave right away and cancel Skype dates. People couldn't sleep more and would have to grab their laundry quickly.

It is hard to think of positive things when you are at the end of your ropes and someone's mistake affects you. These are times when you have to hold in your emotions and disappointments and say, "This too shall pass." It is a perfect opportunity to be compassionate and Christlike in unlikely situations.

What situations in your life call for flexibility? Where does God need to stretch you? All of us should take that step of faith, or let the changes that come our way be opportunities for growth. Always remember that through God's grace and mercy, we have overcome! When we look back over our lives, we'll be able to see that God was faithful—that He really was in control when life seemed out of control.

7

THE MANY FACES OF SERVICE
Contextualizing Ministry
Erika Chaves, Costa Rica

Origins

When 12:7 Serve was announced, I knew it would be an excellent opportunity to confirm my calling. I thought about what this project could bring to my ministerial development and also about the opportunity it could be to inspire others during the six months of the project.

Once we were on the mission field, I realized service would play a key role. The very name of the project said it all! We knew practically everything we did would be centered on serving with the right motivation and with our best efforts. We knew we had to be willing to do this, even on our rest days, and we were all committed to that.

Without a doubt, the key to meeting the expectations placed on us was to work as a team, but that was not the only important component. Another vital factor was to understand that each site was unique. Upon arriving at each country, city, or community where we served we met people with very different backgrounds, customs, traditions, and worldviews. The objectives in each site were based on the local leadership's focus and the tools they had at their disposal.

True, we were limited by the talents and abilities we possessed as a team. However, because of our desire to serve and our understanding of the mission before us, we also knew it was vital to consider the context we were ministering in.

We first did this within our group and then in each community. For example, the first element we had to reconcile was our communication. Maura, Helen, Carlos, Alan, and I all spoke

Spanish as our first language and English as our second; Kesner spoke French Creole and English was his second language; Janary spoke Tagalog and English; Estela spoke English and Spanish; and Chennice, Danielle, and AJ all spoke English.

We decided to adopt English as the language for the group since we all knew it. This was a challenge, but each person was committed to doing this. From that moment we began to contextualize our conversations, since American English, Scottish English, Australian English, and Latino English are all different!

Another example related to language was one of the days we were in Haiti, painting and doing general maintenance work in one of the local parks. To make the time go faster as we worked, we decided to sing. Christian brothers and sisters from the local Haitian churches were working with us, so we made the effort to choose songs and hymns everyone knew and understood, no matter their language.

Understanding Ministry through Culture

Ministry is a personal vocation that uses our gifts, abilities, skills, and passions to accomplish God's mission. Ministry does not happen in a vacuum. It is known or takes shape within a group of people, a community, in a person's country, or even outside of a person's country.

Ministry is daily Christian service, and our model is Jesus who, though He was their teacher, was willing to serve His disciples. He also served the people He met as He traveled through different towns.

Jesus did not think of service in terms of what He could do in the temple or synagogue but in terms of what He did for others wherever He went. This teaches us that ministry goes with us when we go to other places so we can respond to the needs of the people there with the resources God has given us.

For us as a group, taking ministry everywhere was not easy since we had to contextualize our service to seven different places. We were also faced with the subcultures within the larger contexts, such as neighborhoods, families, churches, and pastors. This required us to be willing to adapt to different circumstances. Even though we heard about flexibility several times during our training, during our time in service we confirmed that flexibility is a characteristic a missionary must develop.

Our ministry was focused on evangelism, developing the church, and impacting youth, but the way we achieved this depended on the place, the local leaders' vision, and whether we would be working with children, teens, or adults. So the activities, methods, songs, and ways of implementing the activities changed according to what was needed.

Adapting to the context did not mean diluting the message or rejecting the nonnegotiables of God's mission. Our goal was always to clearly preach the Word through our words and actions. That was not negotiable. However, we could be flexible in how we communicated this.

On the other hand, taking our personalities into account, we learned to be careful about how we expressed our thoughts, feelings, frustrations, and cultures. We wanted to be respectful of the people we lived with, and this required a great and intentional effort.

I remember when we were traveling to one of the communities where we worked. All of the females in the group came from cultures where women commonly wore pants and that's what we wore since they were comfortable. However, at our destination, people suggested we wear skirts because that was more acceptable in their culture. We changed clothes. It was more important to us to show courtesy and respect toward the people we were visiting than to be comfortable.

Follow God!

I learned another thing from my experience with 12:7 Serve. Even though it is necessary to consider the context where we minister and our abilities, the most important thing to recognize is that God is already at work even before we start. This is why it is necessary for us to align ourselves with the mission God has for us in a particular place.

During my time in 12:7 Serve I discovered that aligning myself with God's plan means paying attention to the Holy Spirit's instructions, especially when we are working with others.

Alan was the one who took the initiative in this area. He was always willing to talk about what God had done in his life, not only with us but also with the people we got to know in each place. If we got into a taxi, Alan would befriend the driver and talk to him or her about Jesus. He also did this in the grocery store or wherever people were! This is part of recognizing the divine voice that tells us when we should approach someone to share the gospel.

Taking the step to follow God can only be done if we recognize His voice. Of course, we have to be sensitive and obedient to go with Him wherever He asks us to go, no matter how it compares to our own context. Jesus told His own disciples, "Whoever wants to be my disciple must deny themselves and take up their cross daily and follow me" (Luke 9:23).

Denying ourselves does not mean losing our identity or personality, but it does mean aligning our lives with the Holy Spirit and letting Him govern our lives. Let's allow God to use us according to His will no matter what culture, age-group, social group, or customs we encounter.

8

IS THIS FOR GOD, OR FOR SOMEONE ELSE?
Focus on the One Who Calls
Lynda Woolford, Guyana

There are people in history that we love because of the things they have done for God. Some of my favorites are Mother Teresa, for her selfless acts of compassion for the people in Calcutta, India; then there is William Carey, who lived his famous quote, "Expect great things from God and attempt great things for God," which led him to pioneer missionary works in India.

The others are men and women like Martin Luther King Jr., John Wesley, William Booth, and Phoebe Palmer—whose selfless acts and commitment to serve God made indelible imprints in the world and in others' lives.

But the men and women who really capture my heart today and encourage me to give my best to God and serve well are the ones who—without a well-written biography or the glaring lights and cameras of a television show or even the audience of a congregation—wake every day and, moved by God's love, serve their brother or sister.

The people who capture my heart are like Paul, who travels to Port of Spain, buying two boxes of food and eating with a person living on the street. Or a youth like Dario, who understands that service for God means giving his shoes to another person, because he realizes the other person needs the shoes more. Or like Michelle, who recognizes that serving God can mean using Sunday afternoons to start a Sunday school in a new area, and investing resources and time to make sure children hear the gospel.

These young people and others in our congregations, in our countries, and in the world embody what it means to serve God.

When we Christians bow our hearts in prayer with another or offer a stranger a cup of water, we go beyond the visible acts of our service to the invisible God and say humbly to Him, "This is for You."

This is because God is not as interested in what we commit ourselves to do for others and how often we do it as much as He is interested in the fact that we are committed to humbly and obediently serve Him.

This has led me on occasion to ask myself, "Is this for God, or for someone else?"

For while I can be written about in the history books, and my biography changed into a screenplay, I want at the end of my life to stand before God and hear, "Well done, my good and faithful servant" (Matt. 25:21, NLT).

What It Means to Serve God

As I sat on the airplane, prayerfully envisioning the experiences I would have for the next six months in 12:7 Serve, I thanked God for the privilege of serving Him. I closed my eyes and dreamed of things that I would do in God's name. I was determined to serve Him. But on the field, I didn't do all the things I dreamed about on the plane to Panama. And there were other things I never dreamed about that God allowed me to do.

Both the things that I did and did not do help me focus on the fact that God calls me to serve Him. Just as Paul wrote to the Colossians, "Whatever you do, work at it with all your heart, as working for the Lord, not for human masters" (3:23).

I am sure that you've probably done quite commendable things yourself. You have made sacrifices, preached sermons, visited the sick, run errands for your parents, and the list goes on. People's lives have been touched because of some of these things. But God wants more. All those things matter, but at the end of the day they do not prove that we are really serving God.

Serving God simply means that our service is all about Him. It means having an attitude like Jesus when we serve (see Phil. 2:5). It means that everything we do is summed up in the phrase, "Not my will, but yours be done" (Luke 22:42). It also means we find no reservation or burden about obeying God's voice, as He calls us to give ourselves for His service however and wherever He requires (Acts 4:19).

So when our service is for God, it means God—our leader, our audience, and our role model—motivates us to serve.

God Leads . . . I Follow

In ministry we will use podiums and pedestals. We will be waited on and served by others and sometimes regarded in high esteem. However, these things should never blind us to the fact that God remains on the pedestal of our hearts. We must always remember that before us stands an amazing God whom we serve. When we develop such a mentality for service, it will greatly impact how we serve others. For this to happen, we need to focus on God's voice and vision as we prayerfully consider the question, "Is this for God, or for someone else?"

Focus on God's Voice

In St. Kitts, I was learning to play football (what some call soccer). I knew about the game, but I was not a good player. So Carlos (a member of 12:7 Serve) and some other people were teaching me to play. I made some of the worst passes in history. I kicked the ball away from the goal, ducked from the ball because I could not do head butts, and even caught the ball. But all the time, I listened to Carlos' instructions so I would learn how to play the game properly.

Eventually, I could control the ball and scored two goals. I even played with the 12:7 Serve football team in Haiti and El Salvador.

Likewise, God's voice must be in the foreground of our lives to motivate our actions and guide our decisions. Like Jesus, we must be so moved to hear God's opinion and seek Him out to talk about our lives, that we sign out of Facebook, Twitter, YouTube, and even withdraw from our friends.

In those times God brings perspective, calms our fears, reassures us of our purpose, carries our burdens, and unites us in our mission. For this to happen, we must commit ourselves to the invaluable disciplines of prayer, meditating on the Word, and fasting. These disciplines tune our ears, refresh our hearts, renew our minds, and empower us to serve God well.

It was not always easy for me to juggle work and ministry and to maintain my sacred times with God. And it will not be ideal for you. But if our service is for God, we must know what God is saying to us.

At times, as a team on 12:7 Serve we had to take time to say, "God, what are You saying to us?"

Then, at times God just nudged me and said, "Let's talk." Or at other times I simply bowed my head and asked God, "What are You saying to me today?"

But we have to be intentional and earnestly desire to talk to God.

Focus on God's Vision

Danielle was the youngest member in 12:7 Serve and had crossed several time zones to participate. In recounting her willingness to participate in 12:7 Serve, she always repeated one phrase, *"Six months . . . that's wayyyyyyyyyyyy too long!"*

Danielle was correct. Serving for six months was a relatively long time for the team considering that we left our jobs, studies, families, and friends to journey with God in Mesoamerica. However, the duration of 12:7 Serve pales in comparison to following God's vision for our lives.

It's important that our service and ministry reflect our willingness to follow God's vision. One of my close friends once said, "The greatest Christian leader is the one who has simply perfected the art of following. The call of God is not about charting our own paths, it is about finding the path Jesus has laid, pointing the world to that path, and leading them on it."

This is what serving God is all about. It is about following God and making His vision become our vision. So regardless of reservations you may have for ministering, let your willingness to follow God and to serve Him propel you to focus on God's vision—and not your own.

Only about God: God Is My Audience

When I left to participate in 12:7 Serve, I felt prepared because of all the things I did in my local church and on my district. I was ready to see the need and to meet the need. So in Haiti, I was open for any possible opportunity to help others. When Alan (a teammate from North Mexico) asked if I would be willing to minister to a man on the street, I said I would be happy to help. After all, that is what I came to do.

But he had a specific man in mind. Smiling broadly, he pointed at a man and said, "But you have to do it!"

"Me?" I exclaimed.

I looked at the man Alan proposed that I help. He could not walk, because one of his legs was severely slashed at his knee and filled with pus. He navigated the busy, dusty street with his hands.

I looked up from the man, to see Alan beaming at me.

"Do you want to help him?" he asked.

I looked at the man again and apprehensively said, "Yes."

We dashed to the house where we were staying to get supplies. As we returned my focus was not on the man, not on God, but on me.

I began to whisper a prayer, wondering how this stranger would respond to me. When we reached the market square where the man had been moving on his hands, he was not there. We asked the vendors where he'd gone. My nervousness vanished and I began to focus on the man. We walked and searched until it was dark, and we never found him.

As we returned to the house, I thought about everything that had happened that day. In my memory I saw the man's face and his wound. I remembered the people who passed him, ignoring him.

And I remembered me.

Even though I saw him, my heart was not moved with Jesus' compassion to help him. In that moment God reaffirmed that He had called me to serve Him. My service was not based on who I was called to serve, or with whom, nor who was watching. My service was to focus on God.

When we are really serving God, He becomes the center of everything we do; and the pleasure and joy comes from the fact that we are serving Him. It does not matter how many people are watching us, or what we are called to do. What matters is that God is looking at us.

It is like we are on a stage performing, and though everyone in the audience approves of us, not until God gives His standing ovation do we bow with the elation and contentment that we are being faithful workers in His service.

This is helpful to remember as we serve, because it encourages us to nurture our hearts for service even when others are not looking. It means that even when we are tired, we will press on because God watches as we serve on-stage for Him. It means that even in the least desirable tasks, we will find fulfillment because our service is for God's glory. And God will say, "Truly I tell you, whatever you did for one of the least of these brothers and sisters of mine, you did for me" (Matt. 25:40).

Service like Jesus: He Is Our Role Model

Jesus is my role model. This phrase can never be overdone. If our service is really for God, then it has to reflect Jesus. In the Gospels, Jesus modeled a picture He calls us to emulate.

What did that attitude look like? If Jesus had Instagram, He would be in a picture helping a leper, healing the sick, feeding the hungry, praying for His disciples or, most amazingly, bleeding on a cross. His example was primarily one of love, humility, and service (Phil. 2:5-11). We cannot boast about serving like God until we live His style of compassion, love, and humility.

During our time in Haiti, Chennice beautifully explained this concept of Christlike service when she used her hands to wash, massage, and cream the feet of a youth leader during a leaders' training session in the South District of Haiti.

The group was stunned and giggled as they attentively watched during the exercise. When she was finished, she got up, thanked the young man for his cooperation, and said in a beautiful Scottish accent, "Servant leadership means I must be willing to wash my brother's feet."

This surprised the group of young leaders that day. This also surprised Jesus' disciples. But what if it never surprises those we lead when we decide to wash their feet or serve them a meal, because they are accustomed to our service? Let's daily aspire to serve like Jesus, asking God to clothe us with His love, compassion, and humility.

So, Is Your Service for God or for Someone Else?

During 12:7 Serve, in simple, everyday tasks like sweeping a church and making dinner for one another God reminded us that our service is for Him. Also in the midst of sickness and fatigue, when we were asked to do something for God, He said, "It's not about the sacrifice; it's about Me."

And after a particularly commendable act of service, God's voice came once again, reminding us that His approval and His commendation matters more than the "well dones" of those around us.

In those moments, God clarified that service for Him is not about what we do or sacrifices we make—but it is about God.

What is God saying to you today? Or what would He say about your service? Do you follow God's leadership as you serve? Does your service reflect Jesus' style? Will you hear, "Well done, my good and faithful servant"?

These are all important questions for you to answer; and I trust that you will be able to say, "My service is for God!"

9

THE IDIOT AT THE RESTAURANT

Service vs. Serve Us

Joel Tooley

We had waited fifteen minutes to be seated at a table and another ten before the server came to take our order. This somewhat-fast-food restaurant was not turning out to be a place that emphasizes the word "fast." Thirty minutes later we received our food . . . two small hamburgers and some french fries.

Irritated at the unusual time spent waiting at this type of restaurant, I looked at the long line of people waiting to pay their bill and contemplated just walking out—with the plan to return at a less busy time to pay. As that thought flashed through my mind, an older man caught my attention.

Three or four tables away, this agitated man was berating the young lady who had been serving his and several other tables. His words could apply for everyone in that restaurant: "We've been waiting here for X number of minutes. This is not what we are paying for. My food is cold. I want to speak with the person in charge!"

I am a "people-watcher." I enjoy going places to watch the behaviors of people—the drama of relationships and how humans interact. To witness this unfolding situation with the disgruntled consumer and an underpaid, overworked table server was like giving Vegemite to an Aussie, Balut to a Filipina, or Tajín to a Mexican (you may need to Google those references). In other words, I was slightly excited to see what would unfold.

I am not certain how the dialogue occurred—but the server began to try to appease the man.

He would have nothing to do with the pittance being offered to him, whatever it was . . . perhaps a free dessert or discount. Finally, the man blurted out, "I don't think I should have to pay for my meal at all!"

I had seen enough and decided it was best to move on with my day. I didn't wait to see how the story ended. If you would like to know, you can go look for a man in his mid-sixties, white hair, fluent in rude English, and wearing jeans and a dark, long-sleeved shirt. He's probably still there, letting the world know how unhappy he is. Just look for the idiot.

The word "idiot" is very offensive in some cultures; in Latin cultures, for example. It's a harsh term reserved for specifically unnerving people. At the same time, in some places—like parts of the USA—the term is used almost playfully. I intend to use that term somewhere in between those two cultural understandings. *Idiot*. What we have in this story was a man who was at a place of business, a restaurant, and was willing to pay his money in exchange for a product—food and service.

Service: an act that is offered as a way of helping someone else in exchange for something . . . some type of payment or exchange or simply the satisfaction of receiving compliments on being a good host. The idiot in the restaurant expected service. What he ended up practically screaming was, "Serve us!" This demand would certainly not merit any positive exchange between he and the one serving.

As someone who is responsible to lead a congregation in worship, I sometimes am tempted to construct a church worship time to appeal to particular musical preferences; other times, an equal temptation emerges to disregard musical preferences altogether. The temptation grows because pastors occasionally face the "idiot at the restaurant"—those in the church who would quickly stand up and demand the product they have been waiting for. Like a selfish child they throw a tantrum of expectation—hoping someone will address their need. And like the server in the restaurant, the minister—be it a pastor, missionary, lay leader, whoever—is confronted with the decision to appease the disgruntled individual, dismiss their ranting, or to take off the apron and the name tag and walk out the door, never to return to that line of work.

One element of ministry life I have grown to value more and more is the thread of dignity that I witness repeatedly in the lives of those who are committed to serving Christ and His church. One of the greatest joys for me as one of the missionaries assigned to coordinate the 12:7 Serve project was to witness, firsthand, the tenacity and commitment of the beautiful young leaders who made up the 12:7 Serve team. Thankfully, there were few instances along the way where these missionaries encountered "the idiot at the restaurant."

However, one element of ministry they constantly faced was the need to be flexible, spontaneous, resourceful, creative, and quick on their feet; ready to respond to the people they were assigned to serve.

Serving is a funny thing—funny as in "interesting." I like to assume that most people who are faithfully serving in the church truly want to serve Jesus at some level. Realities of ministry life reveal, however, that 20 percent of the people do 80 percent of the work. This is challenging in the local church. It's even more challenging for the global church where we also consider that frightening statement to perhaps be true.

Where Does That Leave Us?

As I approached the cash register to pay for the food we *finally* received, I made a jab at the manager, who was working as the cashier at the moment. I asked, "Are you hiring?"

Immediately, she replied, "Yes!"

My jab came next. "Good . . . it looks like you could use nine or ten more workers today."

The manager's next words hit me forcefully. "We actually were counting on seven more people to be here—they simply did not show up for work today. It has really hurt all of us—especially our customers."

Imagine how the scene that day would have been entirely different had the people assigned to the task actually showed up to work—to serve!

Who would you identify with in this scenario? Would you be the server who is rushing around trying to do the best job possible—honoring your commitment to the task? Would you be the manager who did her job in hiring people and training them—perhaps hoping they will show up for work? Would you be the unreliable worker who didn't show up for work? Or would you be the disgruntled man—the *idiot at the restaurant*?

Our missionary writers in this book have laid a wonderful account before us about what it takes to journey through Christ's kingdom as one who serves. We have picked up tools along the way to prepare ourselves further—for the next opportunity we have to serve. The stories have given us glimpses of the rugged places that are encountered in serving—they have also reminded us of the rewards God graciously includes as we see His kingdom at work, on earth as it is in heaven.

As you finish reading today, we want you to know the fresh reality that the act of serving is not what is beautiful. The results of serving aren't what is meaningful. Nor is it even that those who receive our service are the celebrated ones.

The punch line of this journey is that Christ is the One we serve—He is the One who is beautiful, meaningful, celebrated. Because Jesus is the One we serve when we serve the orphan, the widow, the wealthy merchant, the housewife, the homeless man, the banker . . . we must serve well. We must always show up and bring others along. We must always be ready to work hard and complete the work the Master has laid out before us.

"If your gift is serving others, serve them well"
(Rom. 12:7, NLT).